Be the Shoe

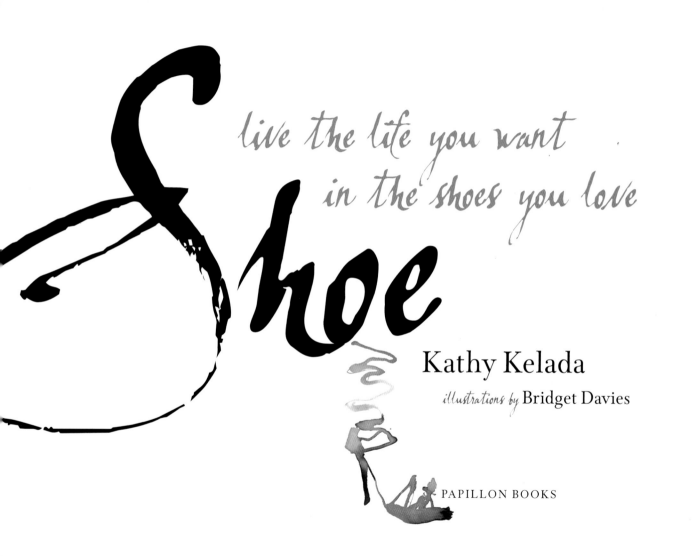

Shoe

*live the life you want
in the shoes you love*

Kathy Kelada

illustrations by Bridget Davies

PAPILLON BOOKS

To order individual copies or for information on quantity discounts and wholesale orders or other general inquiries, visit www.BetheShoes.com

BE THE SHOE. Copyright ©2016 by Kathy Kelada

Illustrations © Bridget Davies 2016

Published in hardcover in the United States of America by Papillon Books.

Printed and bound in China by Asia Pacific Offset

Project management by The Stonesong Press, LLC

Cover and interior design by Alison Lew, Vertigo Design NYC

First Edition 2016

ISBN: 978-0-9976452-0-0

This book is dedicated to:

My  for all the fun she brings to my life;

my for her guidance and practical perspective I can always count on;

my for always keeping me moving forward;

and my for always challenging me and pushing my boundaries.

Also, to my for loving me unconditionally,

and my for never doubting I'd do this.

"I have enough shoes."

—said no woman, EVER

Our Love Affair with Shoes

The Shoes

Becoming the Shoe

Our love affair with Shoes

clog

pump

flip-flop

flat

loafer

running shoe

high-heeled boot

mule

work boot

low-heeled boot

wedge

furry boot

strappy sandal

sneaker

Shoes have the ability to help us reach an emotional place and a truth about ourselves.

I love shoes. I'd go so far as to say I covet shoes.

OCCASIONALLY, I BUY SHOES AND NEVER EVEN WEAR THEM. I just keep them in my closet, tucked away. I put them on, stand in front of the mirror and imagine where I'd go in them, who I'd be with, how I would act, and what I'd be wearing. Let's be honest, I know I'm not alone here.

The power of shoes for self-discovery comes from their reliability. If you think about it, your shoe size is one thing about you that never changes. Okay, you may go up or down a half size over a lifetime, but if you wear a size 5, you will not end up wearing a size 9. I think that may be why women love shoes so much. With so many things that change and shift over the course of our lives, we can count on our shoe size to stay constant. They're not affected by our shape, our intellect, our marital status, our ability to bear children, or our age. They transcend all those tender soft spots of self-doubt and anxiety. The shoes we choose are not an accommodation to our external selves but rather an outward reflection of our inner selves.

I discovered my emotional connection to shoes quite by accident.

After thirty years in sunny Southern California, I moved my family to New England to start a new life. It was a dramatic change, but I think the hardest part for me was the winters.

I have to admit, I was not prepared for actual weather! Cold weather required different clothes and footwear. I quickly realized that my strappy sandals and soft leather boots were not going to work. My suede boots soon became stained with salt and the soles of all my shoes were so thin that my feet were always cold. It became clear: I needed to buy new shoes. Normally this would be a joyful experience but in this case, it filled me with dread.

I looked at shoes and boots but could not bring myself to buy them. The choices were wool clogs, thick-soled shoes, and insulated hiking boots with heavy crepe rubber soles. These were definitely not me! Granted, they would keep my feet warm on cold concrete, grip the pavement when it was icy, and came high enough up my leg to stop the snow from falling in when I was walking through snow drifts, but seriously? My head said yes but my heart said NO!

I resisted for the first few years. I wore my LA shoes even though they didn't suit my new lifestyle. Let's just say, it didn't work out well. I was always cold from the ground up and I nearly killed myself several times on the icy pavement. Finally, I succumbed and bought proper shoes and boots. True, I was warm and my chance of sliding under the car decreased, but I'd look down at my feet and wonder, who is this person? It wasn't me.

Then, one day, a few years later, I was poking through my favorite resale store and I came upon a pair of leopard strappy sandals with two tiny straps and a slender 3-inch heel. I fell in love with them instantly. They were ME. I tried them on and they fit perfectly. The shop owner said she would think of me every time she looked at them. "You must have them. They were meant for you," she said, and I gratefully accepted them on the spot.

When I got home and put them on, my pre-*Northern Exposure* life came rushing back to me. I was myself again. I laughed thinking how silly I was. (As you will see, so Strappy Sandal of me, no?)

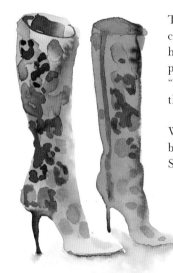

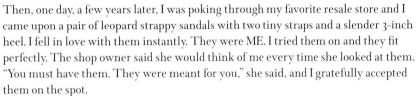

Our shoes, it turns out, tell our story.

Could something as simple as slipping on a pair of shoes connect me to my old life? I realized in that moment that of course they could. I looked down at my feet in those shoes and I could see my L.A. self—lunches at an outdoor café, dinners with friends, running to meetings with polished toes and soft heels. It all came flooding back simply by slipping on those strappy sandals.

I kept those shoes by my bed for the next six years. When I was particularly homesick or feeling out of my element, I'd put them on and wear them around the house for a few hours. They brought me back to who I really was and reminded me that "I" was still in there. I became determined to find my way back to "strappy sandal" me and return home to L.A.

Our shoes, it turns out, tell our story, but they also allow us to write a new one if we discover that *The Shoe We Are Is Not The Shoe We Need To Be.*

Some years later, I did return to L.A. and I continued working with clients to help them realize their dreams or transition through difficult times in their lives. The common themes I hear over and over are:

"I'm here and I want to go there."

"I don't know where I want to go but I'm done being here."

"I want something new to happen, I just don't know what."

My own personal relationship with my shoes stayed with me and I would occasionally look down at my strappy sandals and flash back to those clunky winter boots. But I never thought of applying my personal shoe insights to help someone else's life until one day, I was sitting with a client who was struggling to see herself differently. I thought to myself, could my shoe metaphor work for her? I decided to give it a try.

As you'll read next, I applied my serendipitous lessons about my shoe identity— and life—to a client who was stuck in her own struggle with her situation. It was an impromptu intervention when nothing else was working, but the technique worked! She was able to see herself as a shoe personality and she realized that she could shift her shoe habits and identity if she wanted to.

I started using the approach with more and more clients and the method quickly took on a life of its own. My clients loved the immediacy and practicality of this window into themselves and thus a successful coaching technique was born, and this book you hold in your hands. As you'll soon discover, it's light, easy, and very effective.

Women innately understand that we use shoes to experiment with change and to display how we feel about ourselves from one moment to the next.

The shoe we are is not the shoe we need to be.

ONE DAY A COACHING CLIENT WAS SITTING ACROSS FROM ME saying the same thing she'd been saying for months. She was sick of her life going along in the same old way, she wasn't having any fun, her life felt stuck, and she needed things to change. She wanted change but she didn't want to CHANGE anything to get it. So we kept going over the same ground—me trying to move her to action, and she trying to stay with what wasn't working in her life.

I had to shake things up and try a new approach. I looked at her and said,

"If you were a shoe, what shoe would you be?"

Without a moment's hesitation she replied, "I'm a work boot."

"Ah ha," I said. "So you're resilient, hard-working, grounded, capable of taking a lot of abuse and knocks, and able to find calm and strength inside yourself." She looked at me and said, "Exactly! I'm insulated from feeling anything new so nothing ever changes. I'm worse for the wear but it's safe and comfortable. And truthfully, I can't see it being any other way."

"Okay," I said. "Now, if you could be any shoe, what shoe would you like to be?"

She had to think about this a bit. I could see the options rolling past her face in her eyes. "Well, I think I'd like to be a flip-flop," she said.

Now I was excited because I finally had the insight I needed to help her transition to the next step.

"What is a flip-flop to you?" I asked.

"Well, spontaneous for sure. And easygoing, fun, not complicated, and completely free."

"Do you own a pair?" I asked.

"No, absolutely not. When do I have time to go to the beach or have any fun?"

And there it was. By seeing her life only one way, she had left no room for other options and possibilities. You can't just change your shoe, you have to make room in your life for the opportunities to wear the shoe.

We talked over the next few weeks about her patterns and lifestyle. She was craving new experiences but she was resistant to trying them. Every time she resisted thinking about things in a more flexible, easygoing way, I'd ask her,

"What would the flip-flop do?"

She'd laugh, and gradually she began to step away from her rigid viewpoint.

I thought a little experimenting would do her some good, so I suggested she do something spontaneous—a picnic in the park, a walk on the beach at sunset, maybe even a sidewalk art show. She not only needed a pair of flip-flops but she needed to create the occasions to wear them.

Thus, this simple act of "shoe therapy," and some eventual tryouts with real shoes and situations, led to a whole new chapter in my client's life and happiness.

How many times have I heard a friend say, "I'm going to this thing and I need the right shoes!"

If you think about it, we sometimes use shoes to help us through difficult emotional transitions. They inspire us when we're on unfamiliar ground. They speak for us even if we don't know what we want to say. They can be one of the fastest and most powerful catalysts for self-discovery, change, and simple fun.

We all have shoes in our closet that were purchased for an emotional reason. That sexy f**k-me pump you bought after you were dumped to assure yourself that HE was a fool to leave, the demure flats that remind you that you are feminine and delicate even though you've put on some serious "baby weight," and that high-tech running shoe that says hell yes, I will run that marathon and I will finish!

How lucky are we? We have this visual and emotional aid right at our fingertips, or should I say at the tips of our toes. So I say, *use* it to your best advantage. BE THE SHOE!

I encourage my clients to "just walk through things." Our journey, and how we travel through it, defines our lives. We simply walk through each experience, each day, until we reach the end of the road. This does not, however, mean we have to wear the same pair of shoes!

A change of shoes can change your perspective and ulitmately may change your life.

You're about to discover the Shoe you are, or maybe the shoe you are meant to be.

OVER A PERIOD OF TWELVE YEARS, I honed an initial list of more than forty shoe categories down to the essential fourteen Shoe Profiles featured in *Be the Shoe*. These iconic styles get to the heart of our inner selves and are loosely aligned with personality types and values that have universal resonance.

Are you a sexy Strappy Sandal, a determined black Boot, a focused Flat, a power Pump, a casual Flip-Flop, or a ready-for-anything Sneaker? See which of the fourteen Shoe Profiles make you say "That's me!" Don't get upset if you don't see a specific shoe here. Try to think about which category your shoe might fit into. If you're looking for a cowboy boot, you'll be checking out the low-heeled boot and if you're looking for Crocs™, you will be checking out the clog.

Here's a quiz to get you started and point you toward your shoe.

How to find your shoe

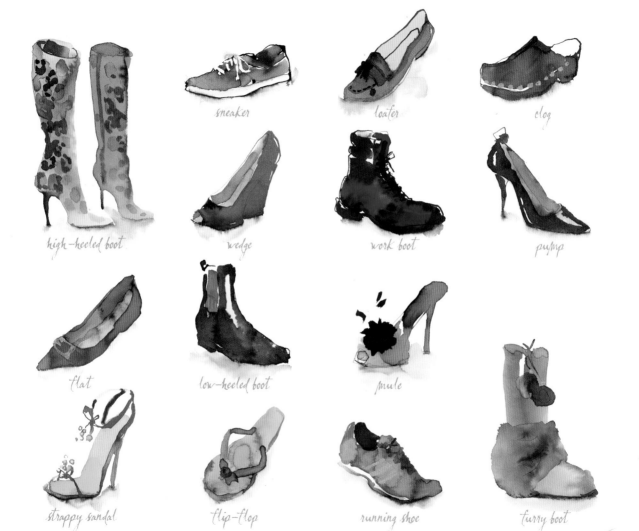

sneaker

loafer

clog

high-heeled boot

wedge

work boot

pump

flat

low-heeled boot

mule

strappy sandal

flip-flop

running shoe

furry boot

What shoe are you?

Have you ever been referred to as "the life of the party?"

When you look in your closet are there lots of colorful pieces and lots of scarves?

Do you have a "dramatic flair" or have you ever been accused of being a "drama queen"?

Does money fly out of your fingers?

Does your style change with your moods?

If you answered "yes" to any or all of these questions, check out Strappy Sandal, Mule, *and* Wedge *first.*

Do you find yourself frequently at the center of attention?

When faced with a problem are you quick with a solution?

When you look in your closet are there lots of designer labels?

Does your bank account have a healthy balance and support your taste?

Are you just as comfortable alone as with a partner?

If you answered "yes" to any or all of these questions, check out Pump *or* High-Heeled Boot *first!*

25

Are you goal-oriented?

Does solving problems seem like a breeze to you?

Have you been labeled as "driven" or having a "one-track mind?"

Do you love a good challenge?

Are you admired for your "can-do" attitude?

If you answered "yes" to any or all of these questions, check out Low-Heeled Boot, Flat, *or* Loafer *first.*

Are you spontaneous and a bit unconventional?

If you see a rule, do you most likely do the opposite?

Is a loving, supportive partner a must in relationships?

Have you been told you're too laid back or easygoing?

Is everything in your closet casual and unrestrictive?

If you answered yes to any or all of these questions, check out Flip-Flop *or* Sneaker *first.*

are you?

Are you drawn to the outdoors?

Do you love to do crafts or do you have a craft room?

Are you the one people turn to when they need comfort?

Can you walk up to a complete stranger and say hello?

Is your closet primarily full of comfortable easy-breezy clothes?

If you answered "yes" to any or all of these questions, check out the Clog _or_ Furry Boot _first._

Are you uncomfortable sharing your feelings?

Do you feel justified in choosing the practical solution?

Are most of the clothes in your closet all one color, and that color is usually brown or black?

Does the idea of being alone not "freak you out" but elicit a sigh of relief?

If you answered "yes" to one or more of these questions, check out the Work Boot _or_ Running Shoe _first._

Now it's time to explore the shoes.

Go right for the shoe you think you are or use answer(s) from the quiz you just took to lead you to your best match(es). You can also flip through the pictures and see if one specific shoe calls out to you. Then lift up the flap and read the description. A clue to your shoe may come from looking at the lifestyle traits that follow each shoe's description. Whether its friends, love, style, or money, see if the description resonates with you. If the shoe doesn't feel quite right, choose another.

Rather, your shoe may be inside you waiting to be set free. It may be the shoe that shows up every day to accomplish the tasks in your life, or the one sitting in your closet in a shoebox that only comes out in private, in front of your dressing mirror. If your shoe is in your closet, bravo! If not, maybe a little shoe shopping is in your future.

You're
true shoe
may not be the shoe
you think you are.

Once you identify *your shoe*, try to find your friends, your sister, or your boss as you read through all fourteen of the shoe profiles. Most likely, you'll recognize their shoe immediately. Then, think about how you all interact. For example: I call on my work boot friend when I need to look at things sensibly and my flip-flop buddy is always available at the last minute to catch a movie or dinner. My loafer friend longs to be a strappy sandal and I think that's why we get along so well. She helps me stay on track and I give her the chance to live vicariously through my adventures.

You will start to see how we are all interconnected and how each of our shoe types creates it's own dynamic when we are at work or just getting together for a fun evening. Just remember, that furry boot could have an inner pump just waiting to leap out and take charge!

Be sure you pay attention to Her Missteps for each shoe, too. Taken too far, even the best shoe can create blisters in our relationships.

Here we go.

As common as an old shoe.

(Seriously? Not likely in these Manolos.)

*S*he is a **carefree spirit**. She rarely lets things bother her and she doesn't dwell on things too long. Her manner shouldn't be confused with being careless or insensitive. On the contrary, she feels things deeply, but **her optimism** allows her to find the positive outcome. She can create a strategy in the moment and carry it through almost effortlessly. She **loves beautiful things** and cannot pass by something that catches her eye without slowing down and taking notice. She **collects beautiful things** and surrounds herself with them whenever possible.

Strappy Sandal

Her essence is creativity and it makes itself known in a variety of ways. This

creativity may be expressed in rearranging the furniture for the umpteenth time, taking a run-down shop and turning it into an **eclectic** boutique, or coming up with the perfect idea for a getaway with her best friends.

She is not a fan of long-range goals because she doesn't want to end up being tied down. People flock to her and love being around her. **She's so much fun!**

IN RELATIONSHIPS: Charm her if you hope to keep her. She expects to be romanced, but don't get too possessive or you'll lose her. She loves with deep emotion but sees flirting as a harmless indulgence. She is an uninhibited lover and asks for nothing less in return. Her friends adore her and would walk through fire for her because they know she'd do the same for them.

IN THE WORKPLACE: She is most likely an entrepreneur. Working for herself is her preference. Her work always has a playful touch to it. She is a hard worker and produces great results but that doesn't mean there can't be some fun along the way. She may do the unexpected, like arranging afternoon ten-minute massages for her team, which makes co-workers adore her.

IN FINANCIAL LIFE: Well, she is impulsive and has been known to splurge on beautiful things without giving it much fiscal thought. She rarely regrets it. She values beautiful treasures and places she's been and people she's met along the way more than a bank account full of money. Sometimes the pressure mounts to make ends meet but her creative approach to it will help her find the way through.

IN FASHION: She loves skirts and feminine styles. Flowing clothes in beautiful soft fabrics are her staples. You'll most likely find her wearing muted jewel tones and you'll rarely see her in black unless it's accessorized with a fabulous accent piece. She owns tons of scarves and uses them to keep her wardrobe interesting and current. She never overlooks a chance to show a little skin as well . . . just to keep it interesting.

her missteps

"Well, sweetie, I just don't do mornings. And really, the idea of doing the same thing day after day just seems like death to me. By the way, how did my bank account get overdrawn again? Didn't I just put money in there? Well, no worries, it will work itself out. Life is good and there's always time to manifest my next big idea."

says yes before no • open to possibilities • light-hearted

The shoe is on the other foot.

(Payback's a bitch.)

Strappy
Sandal

*J*ump in, power through, eye on the prize! This is her life mantra. Yes, she's competitive and she's the first to admit it. She loves her life and loves the people in it, and she's always looking ahead. Her goal is a big one—to be on top of her game at every turn.

Pump

Listen, we all know that she is the go-to girl. Whatever the problem, she is usually the one who can figure out how to deal with it, whether it's knowing the right people or drawing from her own experience. She loves being recognized for her abilities and approaches her responsibilities with grace and charm. Even though much of it goes by in a blur, she's constantly aware of the details.

She's been known to overcommit, but anyone who knows her trusts that everything will work out seamlessly as long as she is calling the shots. At least that's what she tells them!

IN RELATIONSHIPS: She is drawn to other doers. She dates go-getters and her partner's career is most likely on the fast track, too. They understand each other, no excuses, no drama. She prides herself on not dropping the details of her life, especially when it comes to juggling her family and a career. She is also the one listed as everyone's emergency contact because she may be busy, but nothing comes before the ones she loves.

IN THE WORKPLACE: She is the woman in charge. Others look to her for guidance and insight because she has a proven record of getting things done and being prepared for the unexpected. She's a challenging boss, but employees know she rewards excellence with advancement. She likes self-starters and innovative thinkers on her team and loves to mentor young people.

IN FINANCIAL LIFE: No surprises here. She's not an impulse buyer. She started investing in the 401K on her first job and learned the basics of securing her future as part of her overall life plan. She doesn't have a lot of time (or interest) to be an active investor so as soon as she is financially able she is likely to have a financial advisor. Her taxes are done early and with minimal effort since she stays organized all year.

IN FASHION: She's happiest in tried-and-true classic clothes that don't need to be replaced every season. It's efficient time-wise and gives her an air of understated style. Trousers, pencil skirts, cashmere sweaters, and the perfectly cut blazer fill her closet. She loves a pricey purchase and seeks out designer labels, even though some of them are "previously owned." Whether it's shoes, clothes, or accessories, full price or discount, to her quality clothes are a sound business decision.

her missteps

"It's true, getting together with friends and family goes on my to-do list, but that doesn't mean I love them less. They always get quality time and that's more than I get for myself!"

caring • efficient • powerful

On a shoestring.

(Money isn't everything.)

Flip-Flop

She loves to let the day take her where it will. She is **ready for anything** and will often change her plans if something more fun or interesting presents itself. **Don't tie her down!** She hates rules and regulations. Timetables, agendas, and budgets are not her style. Seriously, who can live like that? And why would you want to?

She feels best when she's outdoors and especially near the water. There's so much wonder in the world, **she's able to embrace each day completely** without getting too caught up planning for the future or worrying about what she has no control over and cannot change. She gravitates toward people who are kind and open-spirited and away from aggressive, mean-spirited people. It's just easier for her to function when things are more **casual and easygoing.**

To be truthful, she doesn't much care what others think about her because she's **comfortable in her skin.** She puts her time into thinking about how to improve herself and will happily talk about that if you're willing to listen. She is an active participant in her life and **very open,** which is why kids seem drawn to her.

IN RELATIONSHIPS: Be with her in the moment and don't ask her to plan for forever. Her partners may appear to be different from one another but the one common trait is a good heart and the ability to self-reflect and change. She wants a relationship that has emotional depth and if that's not there, she'll move on. If it is, she'll commit with her whole heart.

IN THE WORKPLACE: Her ideal work includes time outside, and definitely not sitting at a computer all day. She doesn't appreciate being stuck indoors when life is happening elsewhere. She doesn't strive for a lot of responsibility or management roles because she's not that comfortable telling other people what to do. She prefers personally owned workplaces rather than big conglomerates and chains.

IN FINANCIAL LIFE: Well, truth is, she usually spends it as she makes it, though she'd love to be able to save for travel or a small nest egg. She doesn't need a lot of material trappings. Long hours and hustling for money are not her things. She understands that better than most—it's very freeing.

IN FASHION: If it's not casual and oh-so-comfortable, it's not her. She loves soft fabrics like linen and rayon. Soft cotton T-shirts and tank tops are a staple in her wardrobe. She usually gravitates to sea glass or desert colors such as aqua, pale yellow, faded greens, mauve, and taupes—any colors that make her feel like she's wearing nature.

her missteps

"I'm really not that worried about anything. OK, my lease is up and I haven't gotten it together to find a new place. Don't I have a lot of friends with couches? Besides, the sun is out, the waves are crashing, and my beach chair is in the trunk. Wait a minute. Is it a weekend?"

ready for anything • easygoing • unconventional

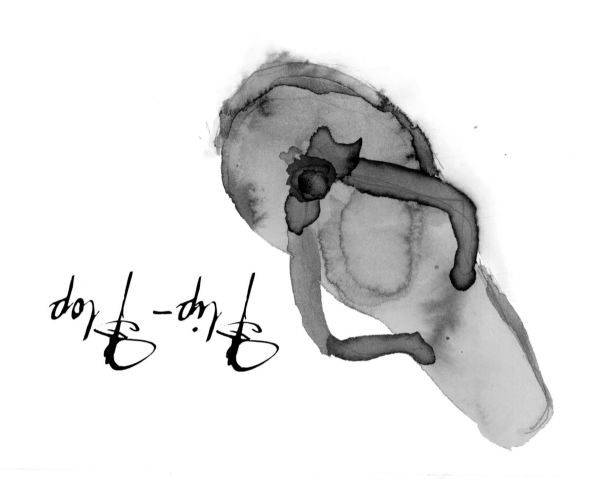

Flip-flop

Put yourself in my shoes.

(You'll look fabulous.)

Flat

*H*ow hard is it to see what needs to be done and do it—calmly, quietly, and without illusions? While others are running in circles or leaping off cliffs, she is taking the necessary steps to get things organized, meet deadlines, and win the business.

She is modest in spirit, but knows she's competent, which can come across as a bit controlling. True, sometimes that take-charge approach alienates others but she doesn't mean to make enemies. She's just pragmatic, focused, and capable, and not afraid to present herself that way.

She's more of a thinker than a feeler. Not being easily swayed by her emotions doesn't mean she doesn't have any. She's a very relational person and loves being surrounded by friends and family. Her role as caretaker occasionally makes her long for time alone to get her thoughts together and regroup.

IN RELATIONSHIPS: She loves having a partner she can count on who knows her well. Usually she's in relationships for a long time because she doesn't like having to start over once she's invested herself in someone. There is comfort in the familiar. Someone who loves her and whom she loves in return, what's better than that?

IN THE WORKPLACE: She is clear-headed and realistic. Her asset in business is that she is a problem solver. She is the perfect person to be working at a start-up. No need to be the flashy one getting all the attention—she's happy working behind the scenes, getting things done. In the most stressful circumstances, she can come across as a bit pushy or demanding, but she's respected and forgiven, given the positive outcomes she helps makes happen.

IN FINANCIAL LIFE: She has an excellent head for business because she sees the big picture. She also has a solid financial foundation, staying on top of her savings for her big purchases, emergency funds, and safe investments for retirement. She manages her spending with a simple app, and keeps her splurges in check. She's not likely to jump into that big vacation or a last-minute concert ticket unless there's a darn good reason!

IN FASHION: She loves to wear separates rather than "outfits." You'll usually find her wearing either a sweater or a jacket. She doesn't wear things that are flashy or trendy. Such styles just don't suit her because they make her feel exposed. She prefers neutral colors—black, gray, and beige—but she will sometimes take a chance, adding color with a pair of shoes … her flats of courage.

her missteps

❝ Wow, I'm so happy I have my life all figured out. Hey I wonder whatever happened to those massage and mani-pedi gift cards in my drawer? They seem to be mounting up. Now that I think about it, why do my friends give me so many of these as gifts? Seriously, am I that wound up? Whatever.…❞

focused • modest • generous

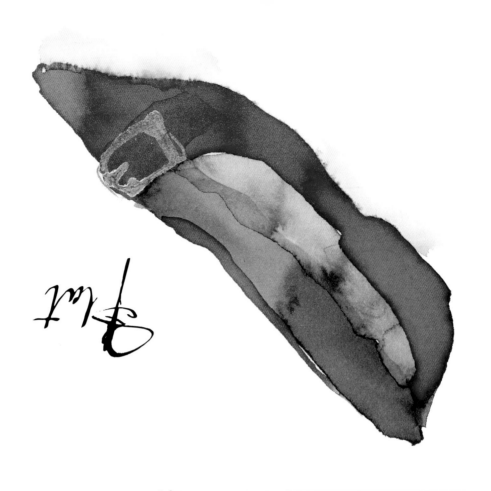

No one can fill her shoes.

(She's one in a million.)

She is a woman who loves being the center of attention and will command it if necessary. She is never found sitting quietly in the background. She is strong and willful and rarely changes her mind about anything. I dare you to try and make her!

High-Heeled Boot

She is confident about her choices and does not appreciate being crossed, though she respects someone who disagrees with her as long as they're up for a meeting of minds. She knows where she's going and will make the best of most situations. You will find her at the front of the line, the head of the group, the first one on the scene.

There are times when her confidence is a bit overwhelming to friends and family, but she's okay with that. And they are, too. You see, she gets things done. Her bossiness can be a relief. She arranges dinners, helps with complicated guest lists (including, or excluding, exes), takes on risky, high-profile projects at work, and even matches up her friends with potential partners. Isn't it comforting to have someone else take charge?

IN RELATIONSHIPS: She is perfectly happy alone, although she'd never admit it to anyone—except maybe her BFFs. She loves her life most of the time and she's an engaged and interesting partner. Said partner needs to be prepared to let her lead the way. They might dance until dawn or sit in front of the fire with a good glass of wine. Whether it's a night on the town, a day of culture, or a quiet evening, she's lots of fun—if you're willing to come along for the ride.

IN THE WORKPLACE: She is engaged, opinionated, and ready to get the job done. As a rule, she has no problem asking for help and she's a great delegator. Her we-can-do-it attitude is welcomed and she's someone people turn to with difficult situations or problems. She's great at unifying the team and getting everyone to work together.

IN FINANCIAL LIFE: She's straightforward about money and spending within her means and she has a good grasp of where she stands with her savings. She knows what she needs to live the life she wants, and frankly she doesn't have a problem getting it. It's a rare occasion that she's caught short. Even if she doesn't have cash in her wallet, she has plenty of room on her credit card.

IN FASHION: She loves short skirts, long skirts, any kind of skirts. She will tend to dress up more often than most women. Even on weekends she looks put together and rarely goes out without her high heels on. She's not a fan of the, "I just got off the couch and decided to go to lunch" look. In her tailored clothes and classic styles, she stands out and usually towers over everyone else.

her missteps

" Some of my friends probably see me as a bit pushy. Funny, they're the same ones who can never make a decision on a restaurant or movie. I rarely find myself unsure about anything and that includes ending a relationship that's going nowhere. Ta-ta, darling. "

takes charge • center stage • assertive

High-Heeled Boot

If the shoe fits, wear it.

(All the way to the finish line.)

W ell, she's a runner. She likes to keep moving, so don't get in her way. She's on a mission. It always mystifies her that others move at a slower pace than she does. How do they get anything accomplished?

Running Shoe

There is nothing that can deter her when she puts her mind to a task or goal. She is very **focused and determined** and doesn't allow distractions to keep her from her desired outcome. Her **confidence** is the first thing you notice about her, and then her single-minded intensity to get things done.

She is a woman to be reckoned with. To maintain the breakneck speed with which she lives her life, everything is organized, scheduled, and planned ahead. She doesn't like surprises. That's why she usually runs the same route at the same time, every day. **She's very competitive** all the time, especially with herself.

IN RELATIONSHIPS: No surprises here. She doesn't require lots of romance, just consistency. She doesn't want a partner who is hot one day and cold the next. She wants someone she knows is there for her, even if their busy schedules sometimes get in the way, and she avoids anyone with frequent outbursts or meltdowns. She is loyal and expects the same in her mate.

IN THE WORKPLACE: She is the officemate who is a role model for focus, time management, and getting a ton done—with enough playfulness to make her fun to have on your team or lunch group. She's the go-to expert and fixer with technology, office politics, and helpful connections inside and outside the company. On the other hand, if you operate at a different pace or with less singular goals, get out of the way. Her management style is that she expects no less of others than she does of herself.

IN FINANCIAL LIFE: Earning good money is definitely in her life plan. She is employed and getting regular paychecks. Money moves in and out of her accounts quite consistently and she's not afraid to follow her hunches and invest on a long shot, but never too much to threaten her security. Saving is something she's done her whole life so it's second nature to plan for retirement. Ahhh, deep breath, that feels good.

IN FASHION: She will not live without good running shoes. Only buy the best for the feet! Most of the time, she's comfortable in her running shoes and not too many occasions take her out of them. They are a part of her. She loves natural fabrics that breathe. Comfortable clothes, not necessarily loose fitting, but stretch fabrics are her preference. Bright colors, even neon, are fine for this moving force of nature! She will dress up if the occasion calls for it. She may not like it, but she'll do it.

her missteps

" Keep it short—I'm busy. I have a lot to do and I don't have time for small talk. Really, you need that second cup of coffee at lunch? Can't you get it to go? Fine, I'll just send a few emails, check my schedule, and tweet my next stop while we're here. "

confident • goal-oriented • organized

Running Shoe

Wait for the other shoe to drop.

(Oh yeah, it's coming . . . wait for it.)

*S*he just loves the beauty of order. She is a detail-driven person who doesn't leave a lot to chance. That way, it's so much easier to cover all the bases and know exactly what's going to happen. Simply put, she doesn't like surprises. She'd much rather plan a surprise party than be surprised by one herself. She's glad that people rely on her. She has a great sense of humor and laughs easily, which surprises some people given her pragmatic view of life. Frankly, from where she sits, life is pretty funny and if you don't laugh along, you will go quite mad!

It takes a lot to shake her, especially when it comes to someone she loves and cares about. She is committed, some might say obsessed, even when they don't live up to her expectations. She can rally, show them how to get back on track, and then encourage them to keep going. She is comfortable with that responsibility, even if it makes her life more complicated. Just don't intentionally take advantage of her or you're out.

Loafer

IN RELATIONSHIPS: She is a great partner because she basically does everything. She is looking for someone who is comfortable relinquishing control. Her partner is a loving, generous person who is not threatened by her taking control. That partner fully understands when she needs to be alone and recharge. She looks for a partner with a good sense of humor because this is not negotiable.

IN THE WORKPLACE: She believes she can accomplish anything if she has the time and resources she needs. She also has a well-developed creative side and that allows her to bring new ideas and motivation to her job. She's usually in a management position or on her way to one. Her ability to get in there to get results while maintaining a light-hearted manner is a winning combination.

IN FINANCIAL LIFE: She has her finances under control. Even if money isn't flowing at the moment, she has a plan in place. She's always looking at the future: for projects, partners, and investors. If she's from a successful family, she may have well-endowed savings account or possibly a trust fund, but with or without that cushion, her money is well-managed and invested. She works hard, always has, and wants her money to work for her, too.

IN FASHION: She likes dressing in separates. Nothing but the best, thank you very much, but it's important that each piece not stand out. She *loves* black, navy, and gray. Those are her go-to colors, but she also has that signature pastel that all her friends know is her color. She may accessorize with a new or pre-owned Hermès scarf or an inherited diamond pendant, but occasionally she'll throw in a quirky piece of jewelry or a trendy top, just to keep it interesting!

her missteps

" I really need you to step back and let me handle things MY way. You're a darling and I love you, but you really don't have a clue. Let me pour you a drink, fix you a meal, and put you to bed. You're in good hands so surrender control—to me. "

responsible • detail-driven • unshakable

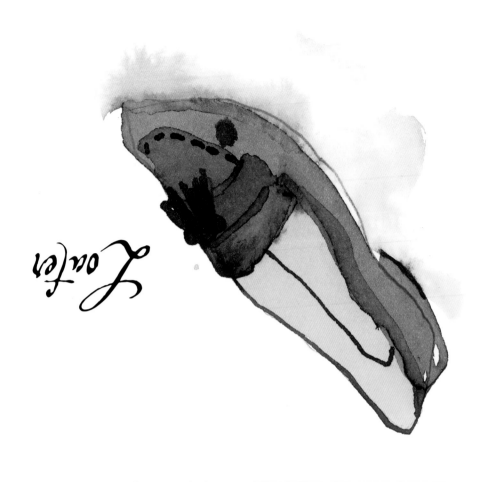

Loafer

Down-at-the-heels.

(Down, but definitely not out!)

W hat people first notice about her is her outgoing personality. Then they notice her enthusiasm and eager attitude. This go-getter appears very youthful no matter what her age.

Sneaker

She's energetic and versatile and moves through lots of situations with little apparent effort. She comes prepared and there's rarely a time when she is caught off guard. Optimistic by nature, she deals with challenges that could bring her down by staying really, really busy.

Constantly on the go, and not someone to dwell on anything for too long, she will be happy to take you along for the ride. But you had better keep up. Don't expect her to sit for hours chatting in a café. Too much to do, I'm afraid. She can get uncomfortable when things slow her down.

She's a great networker so her circle of friends is usually quite large and diverse. But when it comes to her love life? Well let's just say she's loyal and loving but her affections are reserved for one special someone.

IN RELATIONSHIPS: She loves an active partner. She is drawn to someone with a wide array of interests and endless energy who can keep up with her. Together they can cover a lot of ground, see a lot of sights, do a lot of things, and still have enough energy left over at the end of the day for a romantic sunset, or a walk in a park or trendy neighborhood.

IN THE WORKPLACE: She is willing and able to tackle projects that are difficult—usually the ones no one else wants. That's why she's perfect for start-ups—the challenge inspires her. If someone says it can't be done, that's motivation for her. She's good at engaging others with her enthusiastic upbeat nature and can usually get everyone working together. If not, she'll just do it herself, no problem.

IN FINANCIAL LIFE: She wants to have enough funds for what she needs to do in her life, but somehow, there is not a lot left over so saving is a challenge. She's constantly thinking about new ways to make money and if one of her ideas hits, she'll be in the money. In the meantime, she tries to stay in the black.

IN FASHION: She doesn't care about name-brand labels and she doesn't have a need for designer clothes. Seriously, where is she going to wear them, anyway? Give her comfortable clothes she can *move* in—and feel good in. And make them organic if she can afford it. Don't even think about putting her in a coordinated outfit. Separates are her life and they are never all matchy-matchy. If she needs to dress up, she goes monochromatic and puts on beautiful earrings from her travels.

her missteps

"I give the appearance that I don't really care, but au contraire, my friend! I care a lot. I have been known to obsess about things . . . okay maybe 'obsess' is too light a word. But it's all in the privacy of my own head, isn't it??"

versatile • energetic • ageless

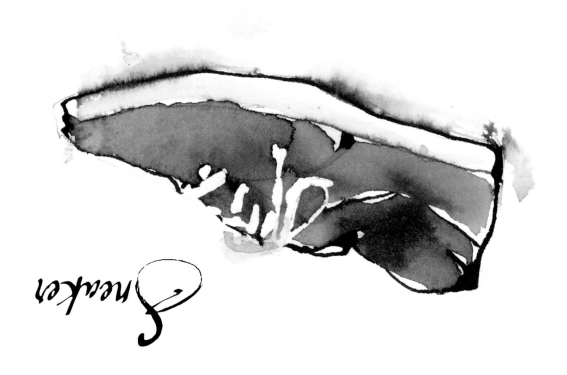

Sneaker

Take a walk in my shoes.

(It's not as easy as it looks.)

*P*eople think **she's fearless, edgy, opinionated, confident,** and in control. These traits are partially true, but they are also the way she hides her insecurity, moments of fearfulness, and sensitivity. She feels the need to protect her **inner vulnerability** by acting the opposite. Truth be told, she gets confidence from this and as a result she is popular and has that dangerous air about her that is very attractive.

She is **determined but not demanding.** She has strong opinions and beliefs. Even though she doesn't talk about them, they rule her world. Her strong personality is her calling card in the world and she protects her soft center by seeming aloof and unaffected by what others say about her.

She **overcomes her uncertainty** and, yes, shyness, by presenting herself as a tough woman who is unfazed by what life throws at her.

IN RELATIONSHIPS: She is always looking for a loving, gentle partner who allows her to let down her façade and be herself. She wants to be understood, but sometimes she's uncomfortable and feels exposed once she lets her guard down, which can lead her to run away. As a result, until she finds the right person, she changes partners more than she might wish and deals with her regrets with her girlfriends.

IN THE WORKPLACE: She is very good at following directions and completing tasks. She is reliable and can really be counted on to get the job done. However, she gets bored easily so may move around from company to company or job to job. She is always well-respected and looked up to.

IN FINANCIAL LIFE: She works hard and saves money and then goes out and spends it on the ones she loves! She has a healthy savings account but she's not afraid to cash it in and use it to take a trip or start a business that could change her life.

IN FASHION: She has a very strong style sense. Usually it's a blend of edgy and comfortable. Her bold choices make her stand out and be noticed. She can wear trendy pieces but she always finds a way to make them uniquely her own. She wears those faded boyfriend jeans with such style, we all want a pair! And she has a way of putting together a leather jacket, lace camisole, big belt, and a slim-leg pant so she looks current and vintage all at the same time.

her missteps

"How did I find myself out on this ledge again? Why do people keep daring me to do these crazy things? Oh, screw it, I'll just jump! Note to self: If I survive this fall, maybe it's time to end this relationship."

determined • vulnerable • edgy

Low-Heeled Boot

Goody two-shoes.

(Who do you think you're kidding?)

*S*he is very social and has lots of girlfriends. She loves getting together with her core group to solve the worlds' problems, or maybe just solve each others' problems. She likes to know everything that's going on, and it's true, she's usually the first one to get the inside scoop.

She's not quick to make decisions because it's hard for her to narrow down the options. She needs to take her time, get thoughts together, figure out what is best for her, and then act. You can offer her advice but don't rush her, or you may find her digging in and not even considering your point of view.

This woman can really throw a party! She has a knack for putting people together and since her circle of friends is vast and varied, her gatherings are always fun. She loves a great theme party and she really gets into the planning. Must we point out she's usually the center of attention? She's been told she has a certain *walk* that draws attention to her. But hey, what can she do? She likes being noticed. Just try not to introduce any drama into her life, she has plenty of her own.

IN RELATIONSHIPS: She usually finds herself in a relationship but, truth be told, she really doesn't need one. If there is a man on the scene, she's very willing to let him take the lead, as long as he treats her like royalty! Her friends are her true support system and leaving them out of the picture is not an option.

IN THE WORKPLACE: She has a natural ability to buy and sell so she usually finds herself in a career that has those components—sales, running her own business, or even finance. But, she prefers to work alone. Groups just frustrate her because she wants to get things done, not talk about getting things done.

IN FINANCIAL LIFE: Most of the time, she doesn't worry about money. Is this because she's usually well taken care of? Possibly, but whatever the case, she handles money like she handles her life. The universe will provide so let's proceed, full steam ahead.

IN FASHION: She loves silk, beautiful pencil skirts, deep rich colors, gem tones, or fabulous pastels. As long as the fabrics are soft and the clothes make a statement, she's happy. She loves fabulous jewelry, too, and whether it's real or costume, the bigger the better: bold necklaces, large dangle earrings, great rings, and an arm full of bangles.

her missteps

"Oh, dahling there is so much drama in my life. Of course, most of it is self-imposed but there's nothing like a tempest to get the blood flowing! Thank goodness my friends just rally around me and someone usually comes up with the solution. These little frustrations take a toll but it's nothing a glass of wine can't soothe."

confident • social • center of attention

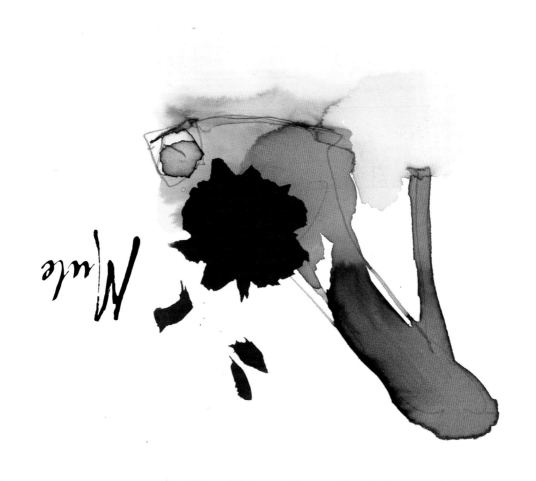

Mule

Tough as old boots.

(Don't mess with me, honey.)

*T*his is someone who excels at thinking things through. She doesn't make impulsive decisions so when she does act, you know that it will be a grounded, well-thought-out move. She is diligent and dependable and rarely walks away from a task until it's completed brilliantly.

Work Boot

She is open to change but she won't change her direction or point of view without a lot of consideration and contemplation. With the proper research, she can usually plot out a course of action and pursue it to completion without a lot of help from others.

Some people see her as a bit stubborn or immovable, but the truth is she knows her own mind and is not easily swayed by the opinions of others. She'll listen, but it's what she believes in that matters most.

IN RELATIONSHIPS: It takes time for her to trust someone and let them into her life. But once you're there, you're in for life. She is self-sufficient, so a partner has to work hard to break through her shell of independence, yet she is loyal and loving and very committed. Just leave her some space and some "alone time" to figure out next steps.

IN THE WORKPLACE: She is an invaluable team member. She works twice as hard as everyone else and twice as long. She is a loyal employee—sometimes even more dedicated than the people she works for. She will ask a lot of her co-workers, but come on, without a big push, you'll never surpass your goals.

IN FINANCIAL LIFE: She is an excellent financial planner. She can usually tell within a dollar or so, how much money she has in savings, in her checking account, and in her wallet. She's not expecting someone to take care of her in her old age so she has at least one IRA account and a healthy pension saving plan.

IN FASHION: She is drawn to earth tones and finds that wearing black always streamlines the process. Everything matches with not a lot of time spent figuring out what goes with what. She's not drawn to trendy fashion but loves sweaters and has been known to wear some crazy patterns. She lives in pants and layering T-shirts, sweaters, jackets, etc., are her trademark. Nothing too body hugging. Her choice of jewelry will always be something small and simple.

her missteps

"Push me and see where it gets you. Usually, nowhere. Just work with me here, will ya? All we have to do is work a little harder to make that dream a reality. 'I can handle it' should be tattooed on my arm, in fact, I think that's a great idea for my next one!"

grounded • practical • always has a plan

Work Boot

Shakin' in your shoes.

(Don't look down, don't look back, just go for it.)

Wedge

K, be warned. She is not afraid to take it on. Whatever it may be, **she is a decisive**, fearless woman who usually stands up for what she believes. She's graceful, not domineering, but always has a point of view. She doesn't mince words or soften opinions, but she's known for being very fair. This is a woman who will leave you breathless with her **zest for life.**

On the home front, she is **the ultimate hostess.** She can create a party almost anywhere and people love being around her for that reason. **Her energy is endless** so she can move from a work event to a social event to a midnight rendezvous effortlessly. She **loves beautiful things** and usually surrounds herself with them so her living environment lends itself to entertaining others.

Nothing pleases her more than entertaining family and friends, unless she's taking on a corporate giant trying to swallow up the little guy. Odds are she'll come out on top. Her stability, and, yes, her **outspoken presence,** creates loyalty among a wide range of people. In fact, she doesn't seem to have much relationship drama in her life. Most of the time, **her life jogs along pretty evenly.**

IN RELATIONSHIPS: Her partner is dynamic and usually as outgoing as she is. They are the couple everyone strives to be. Loving relationships are a must in her life and she expects a certain level of commitment from casual as well as close friends in order to be in her inner circle. In return, she is loyal to the end of time and, once a true friend, she'll be a friend for life.

IN THE WORKPLACE: She has a strong voice. She is confident and sure of herself and has the courage to offer her viewpoint when asked. It's usually the right one, by the way. Her co-workers respect her and will be happy to work on her team because they know whatever the challenge, she will work with them to get it done.

IN FINANCIAL LIFE: While she is responsible, when it comes to money, she can be quite a spender. She loves to buy beautiful things that catch her eye. While she may appear to be extravagant, and heaven knows she's been called that, she will never find herself without rent money! She is good at making a living so it's unlikely she'll find herself short of funds. She's got a guy who knows a gal who set up a fund that—well you get the idea. Her network is huge and she knows how to use it.

IN FASHION: She tends to choose clothes that make a dramatic statement. Frankly, she's one of the few people who can carry it off. It's all about the personality. She loves bold colors but it's not unlike her to show up completely in black. Silly, trendy clothes do not appeal to her but neither do boring separates. And she's always in the most beautiful colors, fabrics, and jewelry.

her missteps

"Hi, I want to cheer you up. Let's go to lunch and then I'll help you pick out some new clothes. Trust me, I won't steer you wrong. By the way, I hope you have some credit left on your card. You're going to need it!"

willful • strong sense of self • outgoing

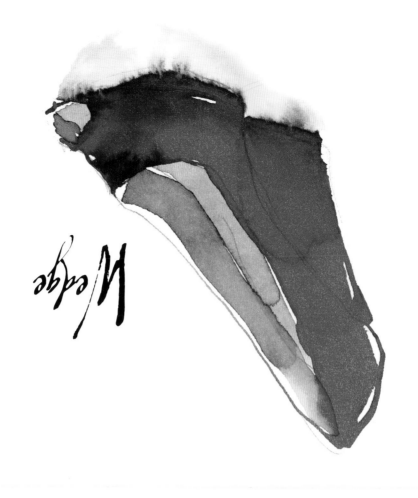

Wedge

If I were in your shoes.

(I'd be going shoe shopping.)

Clog

She loves nature and the elements and feels most at home in a natural environment. She loves the change of seasons and doesn't have difficulty adjusting from one to the other. Just give her trees, a source of running water, and as little exposure to the "concrete jungle" as possible.

She is a nurturer. She has very close connections with family and friends (whom she considers family) and has strong values about her home and life. It is easy for her to create loving connections and she's proud of her ability to love and be loved.

She loves to cook for herself and others because it enables her to bring her friends together for a good meal and good conversation. She has tons of cookbooks in her kitchen and can switch from Indian to Italian to French easily.

You will rarely find her being confrontational. More likely, she will be the mediator in contentious situations, trying to find the common ground.

IN RELATIONSHIPS: Nurturing and loving, she is an open book in her approach to love—what you see is what you get. She is attracted to a partner who is also very relational and loves having family around. She doesn't need much alone time because she gets her nourishment from being with her mate, friends, children, and siblings.

IN THE WORKPLACE: She loves hands-on tasks and roles that require getting in there physically and doing whatever needs to be done. She likes working with people and finds it easy to engage clients or co-workers. She's often the one to show up with the coffee and treats in the morning. Of course, she remembers everyone's preferences, and everyone's birthdays.

IN FINANCIAL LIFE: She has a modest approach to money. Less is more. Everything else in her life moderate, so why not her finances? Since she doesn't indulge in spending sprees, she doesn't have huge debts. A little savings is there for a rainy day, but it better not rain for too long.

IN FASHION: She usually wears loose, comfortable clothes. She will always opt for ease over fashion. She prefers natural fabrics that breathe. Funny, but there's not too much difference between her casual wear and her dressy clothes. If it's comfortable, it works for her. And the colors need to be found in nature, not those bright, crazy colors.

her missteps

" I'm perfectly comfortable with animals and people. But one way or another I end up taking care of them! It's exhausting. If I don't do it, who will? So, I find myself housesitting, pet sitting, and nursing my friends and family. That little voice in my head that says, 'What about me?' Oh, I shut her down with a cup of tea or better yet, a margarita! "

open spirit • careful with money • outdoorsy

Clog

As comfortable as an old shoe.

(There's nothing like a BFF.)

Furry Boot

$\mathcal{S}$he is a very **grounded person** and not easily swayed from her choices. She knows what she likes—and whom she likes. She is willing to go out of her way for those she cares about and, frankly, she's a really good friend. Still, her personal needs and goals are high on her priority list and she makes time to take care of herself. It's important that her friends and family understand this. She'll get around to you eventually. Promise.

There was a time when she would have chosen style over comfort but those days are over. She's living **a free and easy life** and she has her priorities straight. It may not work for everyone but it works for her. Of course, she wants to be socially accepted but **she won't compromise.** Yes, at times she considers being more traditional, but luckily it doesn't last very long.

Her beliefs and convictions fly straight to the heart of the matter. She **is true to herself** and will not let anyone diminish her. She may seem all warm and fuzzy, but she's **one tough woman.** When the going gets tough, **she hangs in there.** Friends look to her for the truth because she sees it. And her ability to deliver the truth in a caring way makes it easier to receive.

IN RELATIONSHIPS: She is really good at relationships. This is her area of expertise. She takes good care of herself and as a result, she knows how to take good care of her partner and close friends. In romance, she is most comfortable with an honest, loving person who enjoys sitting in front of the fire with a glass of wine and a soft cozy comforter to keep warm.

IN THE WORKPLACE: People like her. She's a great team player if you give her a little time and space to think and hear her inner voice. If all else fails, she could lead a project, but she's much happier being one of the group and not having all the responsibility on her shoulders.

IN FINANCIAL LIFE: She's not the greatest with her finances, but most of the time she manages to keep herself in the black. She doesn't need a lot of expendable income, but her self-care regimens are non-negotiable so she tries to be sure there's enough money for those. She keeps promising herself to start saving for that rainy day but never quite gets there.

IN FASHION: She likes a lot of looks as long as they're casual. She's comfortable in shorts and a T-shirt, a short skirt and a puffy vest, or even sweats. Just don't make her dress up in something traditional, like a suit or blazer because she won't be happy.

her missteps

❝What part of 'I'm not available' did you not get? I have a yoga class this morning, a massage later, and I need my eight hours of sleep to feel ready for action. Of course, I want to see you, but it's going to have to fit in to my day. Love you sweetie—hey, why don't we get that mani-pedi together?❞

independent • outgoing • truthful

Becoming
the Shoe

The closet doesn't lie.

Here is where your
true shoe lives.

Did you find your shoe?

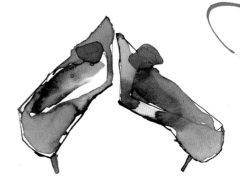

YOU'LL KNOW IF YOU'VE FOUND IT because it will resonate with who you truly are. Your shoe should feel comfortable in its description, but more important, it should feel comfortable on your foot, so once you own your shoe, you can walk with more ease through your life.

Did your best friend pop out at you? Did you recognize your boss, your mother, or your sister? SURPRISE, it may be easier to recognize your friends and family than to find one shoe that speaks to you.

If you found your shoe and you're happy with your choice, congratulations! If not (let's say you feel the Pump is who you've become but you're really a Sneaker at heart), then it's time for some exploration to lock in your shoe.

Closet Therapy will hit close to home. Most of us have shoe racks and closet floors full of shoes we adore, have never worn, can't let go of, or that don't fit right. Our closets are windows into ourselves. Before you can find your shoe, you may need to free yourself of worn-out styles—and dare I say, selves—to make room for the shoe profile that's truly you.

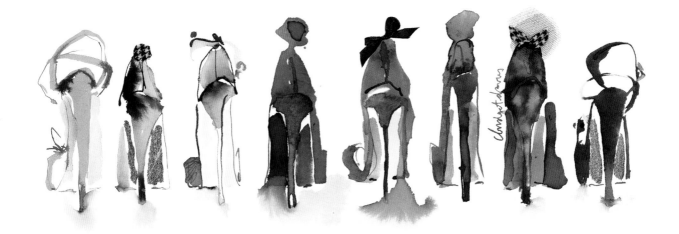

Then we'll have an emotional debrief to see what feelings your shoe triggers for you and where there are potential areas to grow and change. And, of course, there will be some shoe therapy, by way of shopping, to see what shoes might "fit" you and your life with some experiments to encourage you to make the most of your shoe choice and have a little fun in the process.

But let's start with your closet for clues. If more than one shoe seems "right" to you, since we have many shoes we can be from time to time, it may be time to do a bit of investigating.

The closet doesn't lie. Here is where your true shoe lives.

It just may be that your shoe is sitting neglected and overlooked while you trot out all the other shoes that serve your day-to-day life.

Are there shoes in boxes you never wear?

Is it because they touch some inner you but don't suit your lifestyle? Well, that shoe may be too high for your current mate or it may be too funky for your current lifestyle. Or it just may be the real you.

Do you see where I'm going here? You need to lay out every pair and make a shoe assessment.

Here's how . . .

First, you need to group your shoes.

Put all the high shoes in one pile and low pairs in another. Or maybe casual in one grouping and fancy evening shoes in another. You might see what happens when you put the shoes you wear all the time in one group and those never worn, in another. As for those hard-to-get-rid-of sentimental shoes, they could go in another grouping.

You will see some patterns when you get all the shoes in front of you and the groupings will become obvious.

Shoes can help us reach an emotional place within ourselves. Finding the clue to YOUR shoe—and truth—may be sitting in your closet right now.

Next, you need to ask yourself some questions.

How many pairs are hardly ever worn?

How many pairs are worn practically every day?

How many pairs were purchased for an emotional reason?

How many pairs were worn once for an event and never worn again?

How many pairs do you pull out day in and day out because they just fit your life?

How many pairs do you cling to because they are attached to an event in your life?

Then observe the groups and look for patterns.

There are signs here, you just have to look for them. Try to analyze groups. Some of us will have larger groups than others. (You know who you are!)

Do you think you're one type of shoe, but you have one, two, or none of that type in your closet? (If you think you're a Pump but don't have a single pair in your closet, something's not adding up.)

On the other hand, do you have lots of pairs of one type of shoe, even though it doesn't fit the profile you've identified? (If you don't believe you're a Running Shoe but it looks like most of your shoes fall into this category and it's the shoe you're in most of the time, you might want to reconsider.)

Are there lots of shoes in the day-to-day group or just one worn out pair?

Is the "emotional buy" group bigger than the practical group?

Be honest about what you see. Are there a whole lot of "memory shoes" taking up tons of space in your closet? Consider replacing them with new shoes and making new memories!

Are the memory shoes taking up a lot of space in your closet that could be filled with new shoes and new adventures?

Whoa.

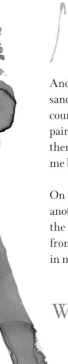

I have done this closet assessment.

And the truth comes out: I will admit here that I have held onto: my leopard strappy sandals, the first pair of sandals I purchased in Greece, my wedding shoes, and of course my feather boa slippers from a romantic interlude, oh yeah. I also cling to a pair of suede boots I used to wear with short skirts and shorter tops. I will never wear them again but I just can't part with them either because just looking at them takes me back to younger, carefree times.

On the other hand, I've tossed out dozens of pairs of worn-out strappy sandals from another era and sky-high wedge boots that were never my thing, but seemed like the trend I couldn't pass up. I've also jettisoned the rubber-crepe soled boots and clogs from my Northern Exposure years. Getting rid of these shoes and boots makes room in my closet for new shoes and new adventures!

What is your Closet Therapy telling you?

Is your
inner shoe
hiding
in plain sight?

It's a *Shoe feeling.*

DO YOU THINK YOU'VE FOUND YOUR SHOE? OK, let's see how good it feels.

For each question on the next few pages, think about whether your answer makes you happy, sad, or anxious. The takeaway here is *awareness*. Awareness is 80 percent of change, choices make up the next 10 percent, and action is the final 10 percent push into a new situation, a new outlook, even a new life. We cannot act effectively until we know, so we should not expect a different result.

Review your answers and add up all the happy, sad, and anxious responses. Be honest with yourself. We're going for awareness here and it won't come from deceiving yourself. You can fool others but come on, what's the point of fooling yourself?

How does your

When you think about being this shoe, does it make you feel...

☐ *happy* ☐ *sad* ☐ *anxious*

If you didn't find your shoe or you had trouble identifying with one shoe, does that make you feel...

☐ *happy* ☐ *sad* ☐ *anxious*

You know your shoe, but you can't be this shoe in your life as it is today. Does that make you feel...

☐ *happy* ☐ *sad* ☐ *anxious*

If an occasion arises that requires you to wear a different shoe, does that make you feel...

☐ *happy* ☐ *sad* ☐ *anxious*

shoe feel?

Wearing your shoe in an unfamiliar circumstance makes you feel...

☐ *happy* ☐ *sad* ☐ *anxious*

You know your shoe is *not* appropriate for an event but you choose to wear it anyway—like running shoes at a fancy dinner party or pumps at a kids birthday party. Does this make you feel...

☐ *happy* ☐ *sad* ☐ *anxious*

The thought that you may have been living in the wrong shoe all this time makes you feel...

☐ *happy* ☐ *sad* ☐ *anxious*

You're constantly changing your shoes, experimenting and looking for your perfect fit. This makes you feel...

☐ *happy* ☐ *sad* ☐ *anxious*

Mostly "happy" answers:

Congratulations! Your shoe aligns with your life. You can switch to other shoes when needed, but you know who you are and you're comfortable with that. There's no need to try to make the shoe fit your life or your life fit your shoe because there is harmony here and you're on sound footing.

Mostly "sad" answers:

OK, there's work to be done, but the good news is that you have answered the questions honestly and you know you're not where you want to be. Now it's time to confront your sadness and realize that only you can change things. You need to step up and look at your life and really see if you can start to flip some of those answers to "happy!" Think about when you're the most comfortable and then visualize what shoe you'd be wearing. If you're sitting on a beach feeling the sun on your face, then you should check out the flip-flop or the sneakers and see if some of those characteristics align with you in some way.

You're primed and ready to take on a new shoe and make it your own. Your anxiety is most likely coming from the "unknowing." You can either stay in this Groan Zone, as I like to call it, or you can throw caution to the wind, step out, and take a risk. It may be as simple as wearing a new shoe in the privacy of your own home to see how it fits you or it may be as hard as owning the shoe you are and leaning into it instead of fighting it.

As I said at the beginning of this exercise, awareness is the key here. There is no judgment. Do you own the shoe you are and is it in your closet, or do you recognize that the shoe you've become is not who you really are? You have the power to change things. You are the only one who can.

This very knowledge opens us up to small transformative moments and we can use those small steps of "shoe therapy" to lead us to bigger risks and changes that lie ahead. I hope the insights you've gained here will serve you well on your journey.

Remember, once **you know something** you can't unknow it.

Transitioning to *a new* Shoe may not be as hard as you think.

MY CLIENT (WHO'S A FLIP-FLOP) MOVED TO ROME A WHILE AGO. She quickly discovered that her shoes did not fit her new life in that city. "I can't wear my flip-flops here," she said in an overseas call. "It's just not done. And if I wear them anyway, women stare at me!"

She was a Flip-Flop but they weren't working for her in Rome. So, she went out her first week and bought a pair of low-heeled black leather boots. They were a bit distressed and suited her causal style and her new life better. Black Boots were her Roman shoe. She lived a Black Boot life while she was there, and when she returned to Southern California she slid right back into her Flip-Flop life.

She learned a valuable lesson, too.

When in Rome, be the shoe.

You may be living in a new city or starting a new chapter in your life, or maybe you're finally ready to be the shoe you always wanted to be.

Trying on a new shoe. An experiment…

Try purchasing a pair of shoes you would never wear or may have never thought of owning. You don't have to spend a lot of money on this experiment … go discount! Put them on and wear them for a whole day and just observe yourself and those around you.

Do you feel different?

Do people relate differently to you?

Do the new shoes spark any new thoughts or attitudes?

Do you walk differently?

Are you more adventurous, carefree, restricted, uncomfortable?

When you look down at your feet, do you feel like you're someone else, or more like yourself?

I think you'll find this exercise interesting. I know I did. I've done this experiment several times and it's amazing how different I feel wearing shoes that are out of my "comfort zone." It might be my imagination, but I think people react differently to me, too.

I also suggest, dare I say, a Shoe Journal? Give yourself some time to reflect and then write down your insights. I encourage you to continue trying on new styles until you find one that "fits" you. It's a great way to begin a transition to a new shoe type without making the big leap all at once.

Your shoe may be where you least expect it...

I discovered this quite by accident. Personally, I never really cared for UGG boots. (Being a Strappy Sandal, I was not surprised by this.) My daughter lived in them. I felt those boots made her appear messy and they made her feet appear out of proportion to her body. They got very grungy from long winters in Vermont, and the baggy pants she wore to accommodate the UGGS really finished off the look.

One day, I had to run a quick errand and her boots were by the door. We're the same size so I slipped them on and ran out. What a revelation! I couldn't believe how comfortable they were and how warm my bare feet felt on that freezing cold day. I became aware of how hard it was to move around too quickly. I experienced my pace slowing, my posture relaxing and my high-heel height evaporating. I actually didn't want to take them off when I got home.

First, I apologized for all the UGGS nagging I had done, and then I considered: Was it possible that Strappy Sandal me could be an UGG in Vermont?

Lesson learned.

If you're looking for a new shoe, try some on. If you always wear platforms, try slipping on a pair of flats. You're not only going to feel different, you're going to see the world differently. You can move much more quickly up and down stairs. You can even lean down and reach the floor to pick up your dropped keys. You may actually like slipping on a pair of loafers rather than zipping yourself into a pair of mile-high boots.

All it takes is a little shoe shopping to find your shoe—and a fifteen-minute experiment to walk a mile in a potential new you.

Taking life *in Stride*

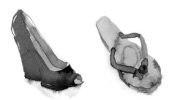

WHEREVER YOU ARE ON YOUR LIFE JOURNEY, it's time to begin embracing all the characteristics that go with your shoe and to try each day to be more like it. It's time to become your shoe.

Get out there, Wedge, and show us that strong sense of self.

Be the Flat and use that grounding to build your life.

We may look to you, Flip-Flop, to find the fun in daily things.

And we will turn to you, Work Boot, to have a plan when we need one.

No one does it better than you, Pump, when life requires someone to lead the way.

Own your best qualities and keep those tricky small missteps in mind as you walk through your life. Knowing and acting on your best qualities builds your confidence. Stepping into your strengths, and aspects of your personality that you may have hidden, will naturally draw people to you. Merely playing with your shoe personality will enhance your flexibility and resilience.

Your shoe personality not only helps you understand yourself, it can also help you support yourself when going it alone isn't the right path, which is most of the time!

Now that you are aware of all the shoe personalities, don't be surprised if you start thinking about other women as shoes, too. That assertive Pump and that creative Strappy Sandal are out there just waiting to be identified. And once you recognize them, consider how they intersect with your shoe. Could you use a Clog friend to get you outdoors more often? Would a Pump help you navigate that delicate legal problem? And from time to time don't we all need a Low-Heeled Boot to kick some a**? Well, they're all out there.

Consider that shoes are just little windows into your "soul" and your inner shoe is in there cheering you on. But that's another story for another time....

I hope the insights you've gained will serve you well on your journey. Now get out there and be the shoe you want to be and live the life of your dreams.

Acknowledgments

SO MANY PEOPLE, SO LITTLE SPACE.
WELL, HERE GOES....

I must begin with my Mom. She always told me, "Go for it!" and always led by example. Then there are my inspirational children, Jenna and Danny, who gave me so much support, along with notes, suggestions, and pep talks as I developed, second-guessed, and refined the concepts in the book, and my adorable husband, Asaad, who believes in me and who makes all things possible--you, my love, are my champion.

Of course, there's Bridget, who met a crazy American stranger and shared my love of shoes and believed in me enough to create the brilliant illustrations for this book.

This book would not have happened without my wonderful team: Janet Goldstein, my friend and amazing book whisperer; Ellen Scordato and all the talented people at Stonesong who brought this book to life; Alison Lew, graphic designer extraordinaire; Janice Ostendorf of Asia Pacific who found the perfect material for the cover and oversaw the printing of this beautiful book., and Hilary Hamer, my marketing wizard who is out there beating the bushes!

I'm forever indebted to my shoe posse who ran alongside me cheering all the way—Anna, Susie, Patti, Patty, Jill, Marci, Maggie, Sue Black (who created the first template for the book), Amy Churgin (who was my first YES in the publishing world), and Shelly Hutter (whose timely coaching was so helpful to me).

To my family, especially my Dad and my brother Jon, who were always there to listen to my ideas and give unending support, and my wider circle of friends who patiently listened to me—for years—thank you so much.

And finally, I am ever grateful to my clients who were my initial inspiration and provided years of feedback and insight along the way.

Thank you all, for making this work so exciting and for stepping out with me on this joyful journey.

About the author & illustrator

KATHY KELADA is a former television actress, an A-List personal shopper, and a life coach for brave women and men who want to face the challenging transitions that life brings, head-on and with humor and grace.

For fifteen years she performed in such classic TV series as *Golden Girls*, *Mork & Mindy*, and *McMillan & Wife*. She then combined an entrepreneurial itch with her strong sense of personal style and launched Born To Shop, named the best shopping service in the city by *Los Angeles Magazine*.

As a further step in her career and life, Kathy earned a Master's degree in Education at Antioch University New England's graduate school, with a focus on organizational development. Building her expertise in life transitions through her work with the Women's Health Resource Center at Dartmouth College, she designed classes especially for women: Life Mapping I and II and The Fear Factor, among others, along with lectures on setting and meeting goals, facing life's transitions, and retirement.

Kathy hastened back to sunny Southern California when the opportunity arose. She now has a thriving life coaching practice, helping celebs and others of all ages find their passions and make the changes they desire with ease and style—and the right pair of shoes.

BRIDGET DAVIES has been fascinated by art and fashion since her childhood. A British artist and illustrator, she trained as an artist at Bretton Hall, University of Leeds and then worked in the fashion industry for several years. Eventually she returned to her first loves, painting and illustrating, and now works as a freelance artist from her studio in Sussex where she creates paintings and fashion illustrations in watercolors and inks, some embellished with paper and found objects. She has collaborated with Anthropologie, John Lewis, and The Shard, and her work is exhibited in several galleries. She created all the watercolor shoe paintings in this book.

Be the shoe
you want to be,
and live the
life of your dreams.